*ACE Group Fitness Specialty Book*

# Group Strength Training

*by*

*Richard J. Seibert, M.A., M.Ed.*

**CAUSEWAY**
22 O'Meara St.
Ottawa, Ontario
K1Y 4N6

AMERICAN COUNCIL ON EXERCISE®

*www.acefitness.org*

Library of Congress Catalog Card Number: 00-106388


First edition
ISBN 1-890720-07-0
Copyright © 2000 American Council on Exercise® (ACE®)
Printed in the United States of America.

A B C D E F

Distributed by:
American Council on Exercise
P. O. Box 910449
San Diego, CA 92191-0449
(858) 535-8227
(858) 535-1778 (FAX)
www.acefitness.org


*Managing Editor:* Daniel Green
*Design:* Karen McGuire
*Production:* Glenn Valentine
*Manager of Publications:* Christine J. Ekeroth
*Associate Editor:* Joy Keller
*Index:* Bonny McLaughlin
*Model:* Paul Ainsworth and Valerie Gardner

Acknowledgments:
Thanks to the entire American Council on Exercise staff for their support and guidance through the process of creating this manual.

NOTICE
The fitness industry is ever-changing. As new research and clinical experience broaden our knowledge, changes in programming and standards are required. The authors and the publisher of this work have checked with sources believed to be reliable in their efforts to provide information that is complete and generally in accord with the standards accepted at the time of publication. However, in view of the possibility of human error or changes in industry standards, neither the authors nor the publisher nor any other party who has been involved in the preparation or publication of this work warrants that the information contained herein is in every respect accurate or complete, and they are not responsible for any errors or omissions or the results obtained from the use of such information. Readers are encouraged to confirm the information contained herein with other sources.

# REVIEWERS

**Frank Butterfield** has trained groups and individuals in 18 countries and spoken around the world on topics from personal motivation to training and instructing. He has served as chairman of the Professional Development Committee for ACE, taught as adjunct faculty at Clark County Community College, and been quoted by *Men's Fitness*, *Club Industry Today*, and *ACE Certified News*. Butterfield is a coach, fitness instructor, personal trainer, and member of the Advisory Board at the Las Vegas Athletic Clubs.

**Mark Cibrario, C.S.C.S.,** is owner of The Trainers Club, a personal training studio in Northbrook, Ill., and serves as a consultant to Spri Products and Harbinger. He is an NSCA- and ACE-certified Personal Trainer, a certified strength conditioning specialist through the NSCA, and a level 2 CHEK practitioner. Cibrario has co-produced 10 videos on strength training, authored two books for Spri Products, and written on topics including program design for strength training, injury prevention, and post-injury fitness.

# TABLE OF CONTENTS

# INTRODUCTION

**T**he American Council on Exercise (ACE) is pleased to include *Group Strength Training as a Group Fitness Specialty Book.* As the industry continues to expand, evolve, and redefine itself, it is only natural that group strength training be recognized as a viable component of fitness. It has also become apparent that guidelines and criteria should be established so that this exercise modality can be practiced both safely and effectively. The intent of this book is to educate and give guidance to fitness professionals that wish to teach group strength training. As with all areas of fitness, education is a continual process. ACE recognizes this is a broad subject requiring serious study and we encourage you to use the References and Suggested Reading to further your knowledge.

# Chapter One

# Introduction to Group Strength Training

G roup **strength training** instructors are challenged with teaching safe and effective exercise classes that will keep participants active and healthy.

Strictly adhere to the following guidelines to ensure a safe, effective, and fun strength training class.

1) *Perform all exercises slowly and with control.* When exercises are performed too quickly or without maintaining proper form, there is a greater opportunity for injury. Also, music selection should reflect the need to keep the speed of the movement slow and controlled.

2) *Know your participants' needs and health histories.* It is difficult to give the participants what they want unless you clearly understand their needs and limits. Ideally, participants should have completed a health history form and listed their goals prior to participating.

3) *Choose exercises that can be modified for participants at all levels of fitness.* In a group setting, modifications to exercises must be offered to allow for individual differ-

ences. Whenever possible, teach to the high-average level of the class and provide modifications for intensity and skill level.

4) *To realize improvements in **muscular strength**, repetitions should be kept low, 8–12 repetitions whenever possible.* By keeping the weight high and the repetitions low, participants can continue to benefit from the progressive nature of strength training. Remember that new participants will benefit from performing higher repetitions with less resistance for the first few weeks.

5) *Stretch targeted muscle groups before and after the workout.* Proper stretching helps maintain muscles that are pliable and healthy, with the greatest benefits derived from stretching after the workout.

6) *Give specific feedback to help improve performance.* Participants need to know what they are doing correctly and how to improve their performance. In some cases, participants may copy form incorrectly modeled by another participant.

7) *Create clear instructions to safely and effectively teach participants correct form.* Use words that have meaning to participants and use both verbal and visual communication techniques.

8) *Transition from one exercise to another using small changes.* Avoid sequencing exercises in a way that wastes time due to equipment changes. Likewise, avoid moving your participants back and forth from a standing to lying position.

9) *Acknowledge each participant and help them feel like part of the group.* Learn names and introduce new participants

to regular class attendees. Make eye contact with each participant a minimum of three times per class.

10)  *Make it fun.*

# History

The development of group strength training has undergone four distinct phases. Group strength training initially began as group **calisthenics**. Exercises were simple and equipment was scarce. Classes were offered as part of sports team training or physical education. A typical class included sit ups, pushups, and squats. Exercises were selected with little attention to safety, and modifications were rarely offered.

During the next phase, group strength training developed in health clubs as group exercise classes. The emphasis of the classes was on high repetitions and "feeling the burn." Participants were attracted to the misconception that high-repetition exercises burned fat, spot reduced, or somehow slimmed the body. Exercise selection was diverse and, although attention was paid to form, safety and effectiveness were lacking.

During the third phase of group strength training, particular attention was paid to safety and effectiveness. Traditional exercises (e.g., full sit ups) were excluded and limits were placed on controversial movements such as forward **flexion** and deep knee flexion. A greater variety of exercise equipment became available, creating program diversity. The number of repetitions was reduced as endurance training shifted toward strength training.

In the most recent phase, classes emphasize functional strength training along with a greater diversity of exercises, formats, and equipment. Also, classes have begun to shift from muscle isolation exercises to functional exercises that are sport-specific and may improve participants' activities of daily living.

## Benefits

Some potential participants may avoid group strength training due to misconceptions about the effects of regular strength training. They may not understand the important role strength training plays in losing or maintaining body weight. Also, in some cases, women may believe that strength training will create bulky muscles. In order to keep exercise motivation high, it is important to communicate the benefits with participants before, during, and after class.

Strength training improves physical capacity and appearance, metabolic function, and injury risk. Use positive statements to sell the benefits of strength training.

To emphasize physical capacity, relate how exercises will help with real-life tasks that require strength.

"This exercise will help you lift boxes onto a high shelf."

"This exercise will help you carry your kids upstairs."

When focusing on physical appearance and metabolic functioning, explain how the exercises will help in maintaining or reducing body weight.

"These exercises help us burn more fat, even when we are sleeping."

"These exercises will help us burn all those extra calories we are going to consume over the holidays."

To explain the reduced injury risk, relate how the exercises help prevent injury or muscular imbalances.

"This exercise helps us with our posture."

"This exercise helps prevent lower back pain."

An effective strength-training program will provide the following physiological improvements:

- Increased muscle fiber size

- Increased muscle contractile strength

- Increased tendon tensile strength

- Increased bone strength

- Increased ligament tensile strength

# Chapter Two

# Kinesiology

S electing the right exercise to target specific muscle groups, offering modifications, and managing risk all come from a basic understanding of kinesiology.

If, for example, during side deltoid raises, the participant becomes fatigued and begins to "throw" or jerk the weights, you can make the following analysis:

1. The targeted muscle group is not being effectively strengthened, since the legs and torso are being used to initiate the lifting motion. The initial burst of movement carries the weight through the rest of the motion with only slight use of the deltoids.

2. One possible modification is to bend the elbow 90 degrees to reduce the resistance and make the participant aware of form. If there is no improvement in form, reduce the resistance.

3. The snapping motion used to initiate the movement compromises the stability of the shoulder joint. Lifting more slowly with control allows the rotator cuff muscle group to stabilize the shoulder joint more effectively.

# Line of Gravity

With dumbbells and body bars, the effectiveness of the exercise is largely dependent on whether the exercise falls within the line of gravity. For example, consider a single arm triceps kick-back exercise. A common error during this exercise is to allow the weight to swing past 90 degrees to 45 degrees elbow flexion.

The starting, or resting, position of the exercise is with the upper arm parallel to the floor and the lower arm perpendicular to the floor so that the elbow is flexed 90 degrees. The line of gravity is a straight line from the ceiling to the floor and is in the same direction as the lower arm. During elbow **extension**, the triceps muscle group works to lift the weight against gravity. The triceps also works as the weight is lowered back toward resting position. As the arm moves past 90 degrees of elbow flexion, it is the biceps muscle group that is working to lift the weights against gravity.

Any exercise can be analyzed to determine when the exercise falls within the line of gravity.

*Exercise #1: Standing chest fly with dumbbells*

**Targeted muscle group:** Chest

**Action:** The start position is with the arms in 90 degrees of shoulder abduction from the sides of the body. The action is 90 degrees of horizontal shoulder adduction in the transverse plane followed by 90 degrees of horizontal shoulder abduction in the transverse plane (Figures 1a & b).

**Analysis:** Ineffective, because the action of the exercise does not fall within the line gravity. The chest group is targeted, but the deltoids are the primary muscle group for this exercise. Because the deltoids create a force equal to the gravitational force, the weights remain in the transverse plane.

**Solution:** Perform the chest fly from a supine position so the exercise falls within the line of gravity, or substitute elastic resistance for the dumbbells so that the exercise falls within the line of resistance created by the elastic resistance (Figure 1c).

*Exercise #2: Standing biceps curls with dumbbells*

**Targeted muscle group:** Biceps

**Figure 1**
a.&b.  A standing chest fly with dumbbells is ineffective because the action of the exercise does not fall within the line of gravity.
c. An appropriate modification is the use of elastic resistance, since the action of the exercise falls within the line of resistance.

a.

**Action:** The start position is with the arms extended down the sides of the body. The action is 180 degrees of elbow flexion in the sagittal plane followed by 180 degrees of elbow extension in the sagittal plane.

**Analysis:** Good. The exercise falls within the line of gravity during most of the movement. The weight and gravity are constant forces, but the amount of force necessary to move the weight changes as the elbow flexes and extends. The force is determined by the **lever** arm, the distance from the elbow joint (the fulcrum)

b.

c.

to the weight. The force required to move the weight increases proportionately as the lever arm increases. At the extremes of the exercise (the first and last 15 degrees of the exercise), the biceps are working dramatically less than at 90 degrees (Figure 2).

**Modification:** Modify the exercise to a single arm curl with the other arm adding manual resistance near the wrist between the hand and the elbow.

**Figure 2**
a. Standing biceps curl; 15 degrees of flexion
b. Standing biceps curl; 90 degrees of flexion
c. Standing biceps curl; 165 degrees of flexion

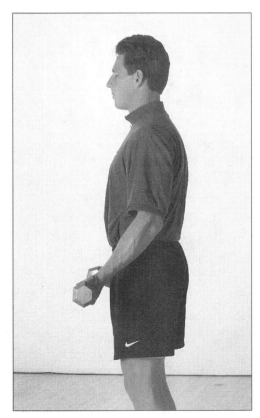

a.

# Types of Contractions

There are three types of muscular contractions utilized in any strength-training program.

## Isometric

During an **isometric** contraction there is no joint movement. For example, an isometric chest exercise can be performed by placing the palms of the hands together about one foot away

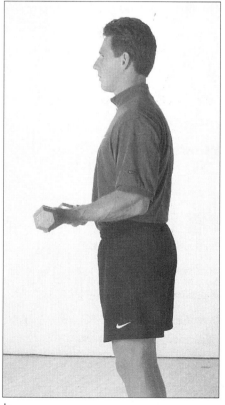

b.

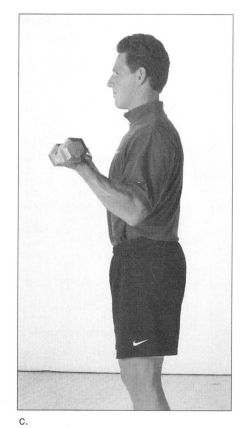

c.

from the chest. Next, each hand exerts an equal and opposite force resulting in a muscular contraction without any motion.

## Concentric

During a concentric contraction there is a shortening of the muscle length (e.g., the up phase of the biceps curl, in which the biceps muscle group shortens as the elbow joint flexes).

## Eccentric

During an **eccentric** contraction the length of the muscle increases (e.g., the down phase of the biceps curl, in which the biceps muscle group lengthens as the elbow joint extends).

### Exercise Analysis

The following questions will guide you in analyzing and designing effective exercises.

1. What movements occur at each joint?

2. Is the movement slow or fast, against resistance or not?

3. Is the motion occurring against gravity or in the same direction? Against resistance or not?

4. What muscles are causing the joint movement?

5. Is the contraction concentric, eccentric, or isometric?

6. Which muscles are movers and which are stabilizers?

7. Does the movement achieve the stated goal of the exercise?

8. Does the exercise train the primary function of the muscle?

9. Does the movement compromise the safety of other body parts? Are nonmoving joints stabilized adequately in neutral?

10. How can the exercise be adapted to meet the specific needs of the client (made more or less difficult)?

# Equipment

There is a variety of equipment that can be used to modify basic strength-training exercises. The equipment falls into three categories.

1. Dynamic constant resistance equipment, which includes body bars, dumbbells, and any other equipment in which the resistance stays constant.
2. Dynamic variable resistance equipment, which includes bands, tubes, and other elastic equipment.
3. Exercise props, which includes mats, benches, steps, exercise balls, or any other equipment that is used during the exercise.

Exercise mats can be used for more than comfort. Mats that can be folded or rolled can be used as an incline bench during chest flies, or to increase recruitment of stabilizers during a push up (Figure 3).

## Constant vs. Variable Exercise Equipment

There are three major differences between constant and variable exercise equipment: elastic properties, line of gravity, and degree of stress on the joints.

### Elastic properties

The elastic nature of the elastic resistance causes it to increase as the band lengthens. Conversely, the weight of dumbbells stays constant through the entire range of motion.

### Line of gravity

To effectively perform strength-training exercises with dumbbells, it is important to lift and lower the weight within the line of gravity. Variable exercise equipment does not depend on the line of gravity, but the line of resistance.

For example, to work external rotation of the shoulder joint, the participant must lie on his or her side in order to utilize the line of gravity effectively. With a band, the exercise can be performed while

**Figure 3**
a. Exercise mat used as a bench during chest flies.
b. Exercise mat used to increase recruitment of stabilizers during push ups.

a.

b.

standing. If the band is held on the opposite hip, the line of resistance created by the angle of the band is within the line of movement.

*Stress on joints*

Because of the properties of elastic resistance, the stress placed on the joint tends to be different than that caused by weights. During an overhead triceps extension, starting at 90 degrees of elbow flexion, the force on the elbow joint is vastly different during the movement. With elastic resistance, there is less force on the elbow joint at the beginning of the movement compared to greater forces on the elbow joint at the end of the movement. Conversely, the force on the elbow joint is greater at the beginning of the movement compared to the end of the movement when using weights.

# General Strength-training Guidelines

## Exercise Selection

Select at least one exercise for each major muscle group to ensure comprehensive muscle development. Training only a few muscle groups leads to muscular imbalance and increases the risk of injury. Therefore, design a strength-training program that addresses muscle balance and incorporates exercises for areas that typically receive less attention.

## Exercise Sequence

When developing a circuit of strength exercises, proceed from the larger muscles groups of the legs to the smaller muscle groups of the torso, arms, and neck. In this way, the most demanding exercises are performed when participants are least fatigued. Also, perform exercises that are more complex and neurologically challenging at the beginning of a circuit, and do not excessively fatigue the core prior to performing these exercises, as this increases the risk of injury.

### Exercise Speed

Lift slowly to work the muscle through the entire range of motion. Lifting quickly places excessive stress on the muscle during the initiation of the movement and increases the risk of injury. The recommended speed is one or two seconds for the concentric muscle action followed by three to four seconds for the eccentric muscle action.

### Exercise Sets

An exercise set is usually defined as a number of successive repetitions performed without resting. Although the greatest strength gains are derived from multiple sets and repetitions, the number of sets is a matter of personal preference and time considerations. An advantage of multiple-set strength training is that it allows participants to repeat exercises they are familiar with rather than performing a succession of different exercises.

### Exercise Resistance and Repetitions

Eight to 12 repetitions with 70 to 80% of maximum resistance is optimal for safe and effective strength development. When performed in a slow and controlled manner, this requires about 50 to 60 seconds of high-intensity (anaerobic) muscle effort.

### Exercise Range

Perform each exercise through a full range of motion, with an emphasis on the fully contracted position. A full range of motion promotes joint flexibility. Only reduce the range of motion when the full range of motion compromises joint stability or if joint pain occurs.

## Exercise Progression

When a participant can easily perform 12 or more repetitions with good form, it is time to increase the workload by 5% or less. Limitations in equipment often make it seem impossible to increase the workload. By using both weights and elastic resistance or by adding manual resistance, workloads can be increased even with only light resistance equipment (Figure 4).

**Figure 4**
Combine weights and elastic resistance to increase intensity.

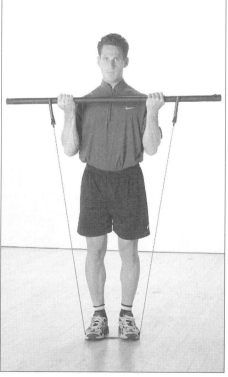

a.

b.

## Exercise Frequency

Because the muscle rebuilding process typically requires 48 hours, strength workouts that exercise the same muscle group should be scheduled every other day to allow full recovery.

# Chapter Three

# Group Strength Training Techniques

The following exercises are grouped by body part, each with a table listing exercises by starting position and equipment. The tables will assist in creating smooth transitions between exercises. Remember to only alter one aspect (e.g., equipment, position) during each transition.

## Common strength-training errors

Watch for the following flaws in technique, which are common to many strength-training exercises.

*Error:* Increasing the natural arch in the lower back

*Correction:* Contract the abdominals (transverse abdominis) and maintain neutral spine. If supine, pulling the feet in close to the body helps support the lower back.

*Error:* Using the legs and momentum to perform a lift; rocking or jerking during the exercise; performing the movement too quickly

*Correction:* Begin the movement slowly and with control; pause at the top and bottom of each repetition.

*Error:* Forward neck posture

*Correction:* Keep the neck in neutral position and in alignment with the spine.

# Chest

**Muscles involved:** Pectoralis major, anterior shoulder, triceps, serratus anterior

**Strength-training techniques for the chest:**

1. A narrow grip during the exercise increases the involvement of the triceps muscle group. Conversely, widening the grip decreases the involvement of the triceps.

2. When performing chest flys, rotate the lower arm outward (supinate) to reduce the stress on the shoulder joint.

3. During pushups and chest flys, horizontal abduction beyond 90 degrees places excessive stress on the shoulder joint.

**Table 1**
**Exercises for the chest**

| **bodyweight** | | | |
| --- | --- | --- | --- |
| *position* | *exercise* | *variations* | *equipment* |
| floor, wall | push ups | decline, incline | bench, ball |

| **dumbbells** | | | |
| --- | --- | --- | --- |
| *position* | *exercise* | *variations* | *equipment* |
| floor | supine chest fly | incline, decline | bench, ball |
| floor | supine chest press | incline, decline | bench, ball |

| **elastic resistance** | | | |
| --- | --- | --- | --- |
| *position* | *exercise* | *variations* | *equipment* |
| standing | chest press | | |
| | chest fly | | |
| floor | supine chest press | incline, decline | bench |
| | supine chest fly | incline, decline | bench, ball |
| | push up | | bench |

*Push Ups*

**Targeted muscles:** Pectoralis major, anterior deltoids, triceps

**Starting position:** Begin on the floor with the hands slightly wider than shoulder-width apart. Place toes or knees onto floor. Keep the back straight and torso supported (Figure 5).

**Action:** Press the body up to the point just prior to locked elbows, pause, then lower down to 1 inch off the floor (Figure 6).

**Figure 5**
Push up;
starting position

**Figure 6**
Push up;
action

**Variations:**

- *For deconditioned participants:* wall push ups (Figure 7)
- *Incline:* hands on a bench or step (Figure 8)
- *Decline:* feet on a bench or exercise ball (Figure 9)
- Keeping the elbows close to the body emphasizes the anterior deltoid and triceps (Figure 10).

**Equipment variation:**

- Elastic resistance, held around the back (Figure 11).

**Figure 7**
Wall
push up

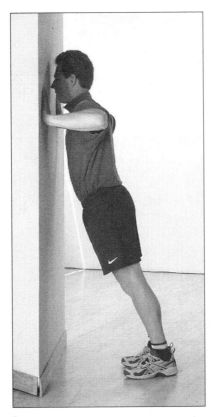

a.

b.

**Figure 8**
Push up;
use a bench
to create an
incline.

**Figure 9**
Push up;
use an
exercise ball
to create a
decline.

**Figure 10**
Push up;
keep the
elbows close
to the body
to emphasize
the anterior
deltoid and
triceps.

**Figure 11**
Push up;
elastic
resistance
variation

a.

b.

*Supine Chest Fly*

**Targeted muscles:** Pectoralis major, anterior deltoids

**Starting position:** Begin supine on the floor or bench with bent knees. Start with arms extended directly above your shoulders with your elbows slightly bent. Lower weights to about 90 degrees of shoulder abduction or to a comfortable stretch in the pectorals (Figure 12).

**Action:** Adduct the arms to the point above the shoulder joints, pause, and slowly lower the arms to the starting position (Figure 13).

## Common error:

*Error:* Lowering the arms too quickly and going past the comfortable starting position

*Correction:* Emphasize lowering the weights slowly and not letting the hands lower out of peripheral vision.

**Figure 12**
Supine chest fly; starting position

**Figure 13**
Supine chest fly; action

**Variation:**

- Incline or decline with a bench

**Equipment variation:**

- Elastic resistance in the standing or supine position with resistance placed behind the back (Figure 14)

**Figure 14**
Supine chest fly; elastic resistance variation

a.

b.

*Chest Press*

**Targeted muscles:** Pectoralis major, anterior deltoids, triceps

**Starting position:** Begin supine on the floor or bench with bent knees. Hold dumbbells or bar with arms extended directly over the shoulders with elbows slightly bent. With straight wrists, lower weights by bending the elbows to a point of comfortable stretch for the chest muscles (Figure 15).

**Action:** Press the weight up to a point just wider than the shoulders, pause, then slowly lower weight to starting position (Figure 16).

**Figure 15**
Chest press;
starting
position

**Figure 16**
Chest press;
action

**Common errors:**

*Error:* Bent wrists (forward or backward)

*Correction:* Keep weight stacked over the wrist with a light grip.

*Error:* Lowering the arms too quickly and going past the comfortable starting position

*Correction:* Emphasize slowly lowering the weights and not letting the hands go below the peripheral vision.

**Figure 17**
Chest press; elastic resistance variation with a partner

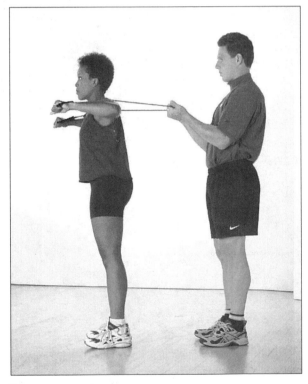

a.

**Variation:**

- Elbows close to body emphasizes more anterior deltoid and triceps

**Equipment variations:**

- Elastic resistance held around the back by a partner (Figure 17)
- Use a bench to create incline or decline modification.

b.

# Back

**Muscles involved:** latissimus dorsi, trapezius, rhomboids, teres major, levator scapula

**Strength-training techniques for the back:**

1. A narrow grip during the exercise increases the involvement of the biceps muscle group. Conversely, widening the grip decreases the involvement of the biceps.

2. During forward flexion, look for opportunities to provide additional support to the spine. Offer a single arm modification to allow the opposite arm to help support the spine. Sustained unsupported forward flexion can lead to lower-back pain if the abdominals (transverse abdominis) are not contracted or if the lumbar spine flexes.

3. During rowing motion, keep the torso from rotating to isolate the primary muscle group.

4. During lat pull-down exercises, bring the arms down in front of the body rather than behind the neck to reduce the stress on the shoulder joint and neck.

**Table 2**
**Exercises for the back**

**bodyweight**

| position | exercise | variation | equipment |
|---|---|---|---|
| floor | supine pull ups | | benches and bars |

**weights**

| position | exercise | variation | equipment |
|---|---|---|---|
| standing | bent over row | incline | bench |
| | one arm row | incline | bench |
| | shrugs | | |
| | upright row | | |
| floor | one arm row | incline | bench |

**elastic resistance**

| position | exercise | variation | equipment |
|---|---|---|---|
| standing | bent over row | incline | |
| | single arm row | incline | |
| | shrugs | | |
| | single arm lat pull-down | | |
| | scapular adduction | | |
| | upright row | | |
| floor | seated row | low row | |
| | single arm row | | |
| | scapular adduction | | |

*Bent Over Row*

**Targeted muscles:** Latissimus dorsi, rhomboids, biceps

**Starting position:** Standing, begin with the feet shoulder-width apart, bend your knees, flex forward at the hips. Tilt the pelvis forward slightly, contract the transverse abdominis, and extend the upper spine to add support to the spine. Hold the weight or bar underneath the shoulders with hands about shoulder-width apart (Figure 18).

**Figure 18**
Bent over row; starting position

**Figure 19**
Bent over row; action

**Action:** Lift the hands toward the chest with the elbows flexing, pause, then slowly lower the hands to starting position (Figure 19).

**Common error:**

*Error:* Dropping the shoulders

*Correction:* Keep the shoulders stationary.

**Variation:**

- One arm row with the legs in a staggered position and one hand on the front thigh for support (Figure 20)

**Equipment variations:**

- Lying face down on an incline bench
- One arm and knee on a bench for support
- Seated with elastic resistance anchored to feet

**Figure 20**
Bent over row;
single arm
variation

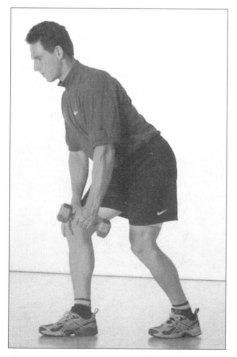

a.

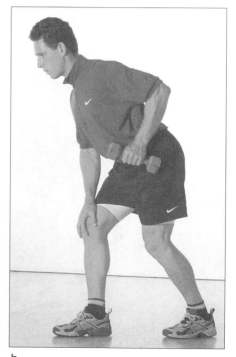

b.

*Shrugs*

**Targeted muscles:** Upper and middle trapezius, rhomboids

**Starting position:** Stand erect with dumbbells held at the side of the body (Figure 21).

**Action:** Lift the shoulders to the ears by elevating shoulder girdle, retract scapulae to rotate shoulders to rear, and relax to starting position (Figure 22).

**Figure 21**
Shrugs; starting position

**Figure 22**
Shrugs; action

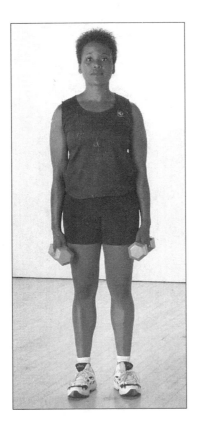

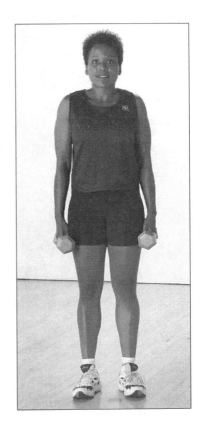

**Common errors:**

*Error:* Rocking or using the legs to initiate the exercise

*Correction:* Maintain slightly bent knees.

*Error:* Bending the elbows

*Correction:* Relax the upper arms and lift using the upper back.

**Variation:**

- Perform one shoulder at a time

**Equipment variation:**

- Elastic resistance; perform in a staggered or standing position with band anchored under feet (Figure 23)

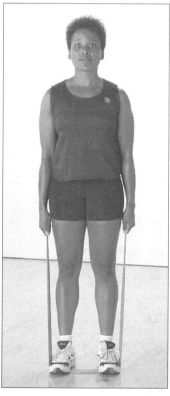
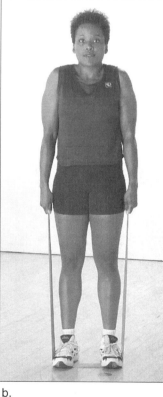

a.                                        b.

**Figure 23**
Shrugs; elastic resistance variation

*Upright Row*

**Targeted muscles:** Middle deltoid, trapezius

**Starting position:** Begin with hands holding dumbbells or elastic resistance in front of the body (Figure 24).

**Action:** Start by elevating the scapulae. Lead with the elbows and raise the arms until the upper arms are shoulder height (keep dumbbells close to the body throughout), pause, and slowly return to starting position (Figure 25).

**Figure 24**
Upright row; starting position

**Figure 25**
Upright row; action

**Common error:**

*Error:* Lifting the elbows too high

*Correction:* Keep the elbows at or below shoulder height.

**Variation:**

- One arm at a time. During the lift, the hands can move forward away from the body to reduce the stress on the shoulder joint.

**Equipment variation:**

- Elastic resistance; can be performed in standing or staggered position with the band anchored below the feet (Figure 26)

**Figure 26**
Upright row;
elastic resistance
variation

*Single Arm Lat Pull-down*

**Targeted muscle:** Latissimus dorsi

**Starting position:** Begin with both hands overhead holding an elastic resistance band; maintain neutral wrist and soft joints. Contract the transverse abdominis, bend the knees, and keep your feet about shoulder-width apart (Figure 27).

**Action:** Pull with one arm, adducting at the shoulder until the upper arm is next to the torso; return slowly to the extended position. Keep arms slightly in front of the face to protect the back and shoulders (Figure 28).

**Figure 27**
Single arm lat pull-down using elastic resistance; starting position

**Common errors:**

*Error:* Flexing the wrist

*Correction:* Keep your hand stacked over the top of the wrist.

*Error:* Allowing the arms to drift back behind the neck

*Correction:* Keep your hands in peripheral vision at all times.

**Variation:**

* Bend the elbow more to decrease the resistance and reduce the stress on the shoulder joint.

**Figure 28**
Single arm lat pull-down using elastic resistance; action

*Scapular Adduction*

**Targeted muscle:** Rhomboids

**Starting position:** Begin with feet about shoulder-width apart and the pelvis tilted slightly forward; contract the transverse abdominis to help maintain neutral spine. Flex forward and hold dumbbells extended down away from the body (Figure 29).

**Action:** Adduct shoulder blades together, pause, and then slowly return to starting position (Figure 30).

**Figure 29**
Scapular adduction;
starting position

**Figure 30**
Scapular adduction;
action

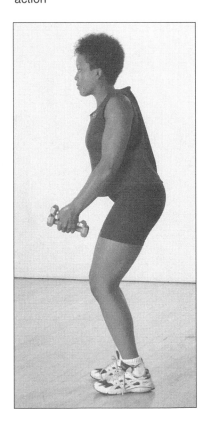

**Common error:**

*Error:* Bending the elbows

*Correction:* Relax the upper arms and lift using the upper back.

**Variation:**

- Single arm

**Figure 31**
Scapular adduction; variation with one arm and both knees on a bench

a.

b.

**Equipment variations:**

- Prone on a bench or with one arm and both knees on the bench (Figure 31)
- Elastic resistance anchored at feet

*Seated Row*

**Targeted muscle:** Rhomboids

**Starting position:** Sit with your legs extended in front of you and your knees bent. Begin by securing a band around your feet. Extend arms in front of the body and hold the band with a pronated grip (Figure 32).

**Action:** Retract the scapulae; lead with the elbows and pull the band back toward the side of your torso in line with your sternum. Hold for several seconds, release and slowly return to starting position (Figure 33).

**Figure 32**
Seated row;
starting
position

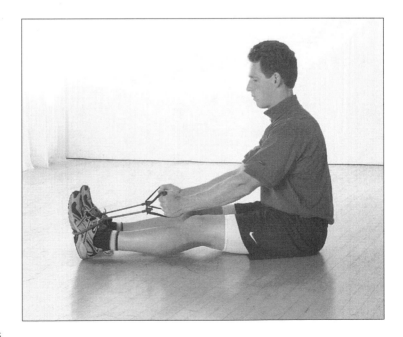

**Common errors:**

*Error:* Raising the shoulders

*Correction:* Keep your shoulders down and shoulder blades in their neutral position.

*Error:* Flexing at the wrist

*Correction:* Pull in a straight line with straight wrists through the entire range of motion.

**Variations:**

- Single arm
- Low row (the ending point is at belly button-level and the arms can be supinated)
- Seated on bench

**Equipment variation:**

- Elastic resistance

**Figure 33**
Seated row; action

**Figure 34**
**Securing the elastic band to your feet**

a. Place elastic band across the top of the shoes, over the shoe laces.

b. Wrap the band around the shoe. Start at the outside of the shoes and wrap toward the bottom of shoes. The band then goes through the middle so that it can be used in a seated position.

a.

b.

# Shoulders

**Muscles involved:** Anterior, posterior, and middle deltoid

**Strength-training techniques for the shoulder:**

1. Avoid exercises that exceed 90 degrees of shoulder flexion or extension. Front and side lateral raises should start by the sides of the body and lift to 90 degrees.

2. Overhead shoulder press should be done in front of the body rather than behind the neck.

3. When pressing over the head, keep the spine neutral with the abdominals supporting the torso.

4. During upright rows, minimize inward rotation of the shoulder by raising the upper arms only to shoulder height. The starting point is with the arms close to the body. During the concentric muscle action, move the hands forward on a 15 degree angle (the scapular plane) to reduce the stress on the shoulder.

5. Rows performed with the elbows closer to the body target the latissimus dorsi, rhomboids, and biceps. Rows performed with the elbows away from the body target the rhomboids and middle trapezius.

**Table 3**
**Exercises for the shoulder**

**weights**

| position | exercise | variation | equipment |
|----------|----------|-----------|-----------|
| standing | front deltoid raises | | bar |
| | lateral deltoid raises | bent elbow | |
| | overhead | | bar |
| | Arnold press | | |
| | posterior shoulder extension | | |
| floor | posterior shoulder extension | | bench |
| | Arnold press | | |
| | lateral deltoid raise | bent elbow | |

**elastic resistance**

| position | exercise | variation | equipment |
|----------|----------|-----------|-----------|
| standing | front deltoid raise | | |
| | lateral deltoid raise | bent elbows | |
| | overhead press | | |
| | Arnold press | | |
| | posterior shoulder extension | | |
| floor | overhead press | | |
| | Arnold press | | |
| | lateral raise | bent elbows | |
| | posterior shoulder extension | | |

*Front Deltoid Raises*

**Targeted muscle:** Anterior deltoid

**Starting position:** Arms start in front of the body with the palms facing the thighs. Contract the transverse abdominis, bend the knees slightly, and keep the feet about shoulder-width apart (Figure 35).

**Action:** Keep elbow extended and flex at the shoulder to raise the arm to 90 degrees (shoulder height), pause, then slowly return to starting position (Figure 36).

**Figure 35**
Front deltoid raises; starting position

**Figure 36**
Front deltoid raises; action

**Common error:**

*Error:* Raising the arms too high

*Correction:* Stop the hands when they reach shoulder height, before they get to eye level.

**Variation:**

- Single arm (Figure 37)

**Equipment variations:**

- Elastic resistance anchored at the feet
- Seated on bench or ball

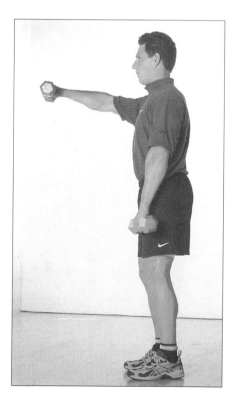

**Figure 37**
Front deltoid raises; single arm variation

*Lateral Deltoid Raises*

**Targeted muscle:** Middle deltoid

**Starting position:** Hands start at your sides, palms facing the thighs. Contract the transverse abdominis, bend the knees slightly, and keep the feet about shoulder-width apart (Figure 38).

**Action:** Keep elbows extended and flex at the shoulder to raise the arms 90 degrees (shoulder height), pause, then return slowly to starting position (Figure 39).

**Figure 38**
Lateral deltoid raises;
starting position

**Figure 39**
Lateral deltoid raises;
action

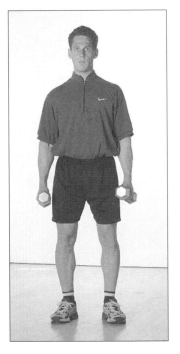

**Common error:**

*Error:* Raising the arms too high

*Correction:* Stop the elbows when they reach shoulder height.

**Variations:**

- Perform the movement single-arm
- Bend the elbows to reduce the intensity (Figure 40)

**Equipment variations:**

- Elastic resistance anchored under feet
- Bench or ball

**Figure 40**
Lateral deltoid raises; bend the elbows to reduce intensity.

*Overhead Press*

**Targeted muscles:** Middle deltoid, triceps

**Starting position:** Hands start at shoulder height, elbows flexed. Contract the transverse abdominis, bend the knees slightly, and keep the feet about shoulder-width apart (Figure 41).

**Action:** Abduct at the shoulder and press the hands over the head until elbows are extended but not locked, pause, then slowly return to the starting position (Figure 42).

**Figure 41**
Overhead press;
starting position

**Figure 42**
Overhead
press; action

**Common error:**

*Error:* Hands drifting behind the neck; elbows drifting behind the shoulders

*Correction:* Keep arms slightly in front of the ears to prevent hyperextension of the spine.

**Variations:**

- Arnold press, in which the hands pronate during the lifting phase and supinate during the lowering phase (Figure 43)
- Perform single-arm

**Figure 43**
Overhead press; Arnold press variation

a.                              b.

**Equipment variations:**

- Perform seated on a bench or ball
- Perform with elastic resistance secured at the feet
- Elastic resistance with a single arm, with the band secured under the same foot

*Posterior Shoulder Extension*

**Targeted muscle:** Posterior deltoid

**Starting position:** Start in lunge position, lean the torso forward to 45 degrees, and provide additional support for the back with the non-working hand on the forward leg. Extend the working arm toward the floor with the palm facing the non-working hand. Contract the transverse abdominis to help maintain neutral spine (Figure 44).

**Action:** Retract scapula and, keeping elbow extended, raise the arm 90 degrees (shoulder height) (Figure 45). Pause, then slowly lower weight to starting position.

**Common errors:**

*Error:* Not supporting the lower back

*Correction:* Place the non-working hand firmly on the mid-thigh with fingertips toward the inner thigh.

*Error:* Twisting the torso, raising the shoulder

*Correction:* Keep your shoulders stationary and even.

**Variation:**

- On hands and knees, single-arm lifts with weight (Figure 46)

**Equipment variations:**

- Elastic resistance with band anchored at forward foot
- Elastic resistance from seated position (on a bench or ball) with band anchored at feet

**Figure 44**
Posterior shoulder
extension; starting position

**Figure 45**
Posterior shoulder
extension; action

**Figure 46**
Posterior shoulder
extension; single
arm variation

a.

b.

# Rotator Cuff

**Muscles involved:** Infraspinatus, subscapularis, supraspina-tus, and teres minor

**Strength-training technique for the rotator cuff:**

Teach participants how to contract, or set, the rotator muscle group in order to stabilize the shoulder joint. This contraction can be done on its own or as part of the starting positions for shoulder exercises.

**Table 4**
**Exercises for the rotator cuff**

| **weights** | | | |
| --- | --- | --- | --- |
| *position* | *exercise* | *variation* | *equipment* |
| standing | outward rotation | bent over | |
| floor | inward rotation | | |
| | outward rotation | | |
| **elastic resistance** | | | |
| *position* | *exercise* | *variation* | *equipment* |
| standing | outward rotation | | |
| floor | outward rotation | | |

*Outward/External Shoulder Rotation*

**Targeted muscles:** Infraspinatus, teres minor

**Starting position:** Flex one elbow 90 degrees, holding the upper arm next to your torso (Figure 47).

**Action:** Externally rotate through full range of motion, pause, then slowly return to the starting position (Figure 48)

**Common errors:**

*Error:* Rotating the torso

*Correction:* Keep the body stationary.

*Error:* Upper arm drifting away from body

**Figure 47**
Outward shoulder rotation; starting position

**Figure 48**
Outward shoulder rotation; action

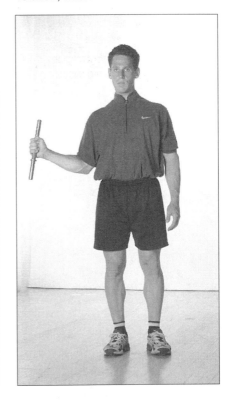

*Correction:* Keep the elbow immediately next to the body, holding a towel between the elbow and the ribs.

**Variation:**

- Lying on one side with weights (Figure 49)

**Equipment variations:**

- Standing, using elastic resistance
- Standing in a staggered lunge position with the non-moving arm providing additional support for the lower back
- Seated with elastic resistance anchored to opposite foot

**Figure 49**
Outward shoulder
rotation; variation

a.

b.

*Internal Shoulder Rotation*

**Targeted muscles:** Subscapularis, teres major

**Starting position:** Lying on your side, flex your supporting arm 90 degrees and hold the upper arm next to your torso, slightly in front of the body and along the floor (Figure 50).

**Action:** Internally rotate the bottom hand toward the body, pause, and slowly lower to starting position (Figure 51).

**Common errors:**

*Error:* Rotating the torso

*Correction:* Keep your body stationary.

*Error:* Upper arm drifting away from body

*Correction:* Keep the elbow in tight to the body.

**Variation:**

- Standing

**Equipment variation:**

- Elastic resistance

**Figure 50**
Inward
shoulder
rotation;
starting
position

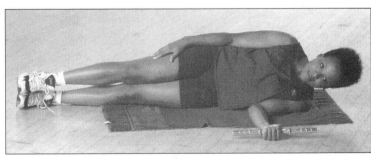

**Figure 51**
Inward
shoulder
rotation;
action

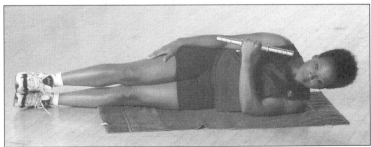

# Triceps

**Muscles involved:** Biceps brachii, brachialis, brachioradialis, triceps brachii, pronator teres

**Strength-training techniques for the triceps:**

1. Deep elbow flexion may cause excessive stress on the elbow joint during triceps exercises.
2. When pressing over the head, contract the transverse abdominis to help maintain neutral spine.

**Table 5**
**Exercises for the triceps**

| bodyweight | | | |
|---|---|---|---|
| *position* | *exercise* | *variation* | *equipment* |
| seated | bench dips | | bench |
| floor | one arm tricep push up | | |
| **weights** | | | |
| *position* | *exercise* | *variation* | *equipment* |
| standing | overhead triceps press | | |
| | triceps kick back | | |
| floor | overhead triceps press | | bars |
| | supine overhead press | | bars |
| **elastic resistance** | | | |
| *position* | *exercise* | *variation* | *equipment* |
| standing | overhead triceps press | | |
| | triceps kick back | | |
| | triceps push down | | |
| | shoulder extension | | |
| floor | overhead triceps press | | |
| | triceps push ups | | |

*Bench Dips*

**Targeted muscle:** Triceps

**Starting position:** Sit on a bench and grip the front edge with your hands shoulder-width apart. Extend your legs straight in front of the body with the heels pressed together on the floor. Move forward until the hips are off the bench (Figure 52).

**Action:** Slowly lower the hips toward the floor, then press up to full arm extension without locking the elbows (Figure 53).

**Common error:**

*Error:* Lowering too fast

*Correction:* Slowly count to four as you lower the body.

**Figure 52**
Bench dips;
starting
position

**Figure 53**
Bench dips;
action

**Variations:**

- Begin with bent knees with the feet directly beneath the knees to reduce workload.
- Place a weight securely on the upper thigh area.

**Equipment variations:**

- Feet can be placed a on second bench (Figure 54).

**Figure 54**
Bench dips; variation using a second bench

a.

b.

*Tricep Push Ups*

**Targeted muscle:** Triceps

**Starting position:** Begin by lying on your side with your body extended in a straight line. Cross your supporting arm in front of the chest with the hand near the armpit. Place the top hand flat on the floor in front of the lower elbow (Figure 55).

**Action:** Push up with the top arm to the point just prior to locking the elbow. Maintain a stabilized trunk throughout the

**Figure 55**
Tricep push up;
starting position

movement (Figure 56). Pause, then slowly lower to one inch above the floor.

**Common error:**

*Error:* Rocking

*Correction:* Slowly lower the body and pause when the body reaches a point one inch above the floor.

**Figure 56**
Tricep push up; action

*Overhead Triceps Press*

**Targeted muscle:** Triceps

**Starting position:** Stand erect with elbows aligned with the shoulders just above the ears. Hold weights slightly above the scapula. Keep the upper arm stationary throughout the entire exercise (Figure 57).

**Figure 57**
Overhead triceps press; starting position

**Figure 58**
Overhead triceps press; action

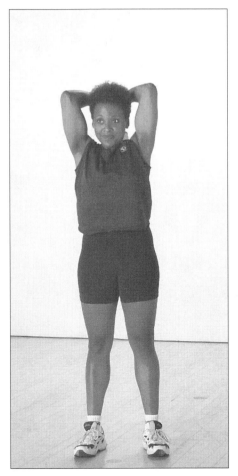

**Action:** Flex at the elbow and lift the weights above the head to the point just prior to locking the elbows (Figure 58). Pause, then slowly lower the weight to a point one inch above the upper back.

**Common error:**

*Error:* Upper-arm movement

*Correction:* Keep the upper arm stationary as though it is part of the spine.

**Variations:**

- One arm at a time
- Staggered foot position
- Tricep push down

**Equipment variations:**

- Elastic resistance
- Seated on a bench or on the floor

*Triceps Kickback*

**Targeted muscle:** Triceps

**Starting position:** Begin with feet in a staggered position. Provide additional support for the trunk by placing one hand on the thigh with a slightly bent elbow and the arm rotated inward so the fingers are toward the inner thigh. With the weight in the other hand, extend the elbow behind until the upper arm is parallel with the floor and palm is facing the torso. Contract the transverse abdominis (Figure 59).

**Action:** Contract the triceps until the arm almost fully extends, pause, then slowly return to starting position (Figure 60).

**Figure 59**
Triceps kickback; starting position

**Figure 60**
Triceps kickback; action

**Common errors:**

*Error:* Moving the upper arm

*Correction:* Keep the upper arm stationary throughout the entire movement.

*Error:* Swinging the weight

*Correction:* Slowly lower the weight back to the starting position and pause when the hand returns to a position under the elbow.

**Variations:**

- Start with feet shoulder-width apart rather than staggered. Flex your body forward 30 degrees and perform the exercise with both arms at the same time (Figure 61).

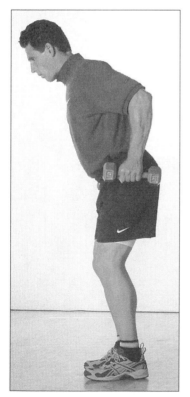 

**Figure 61**
Triceps kickback; variation

a.  b.

- Use a bench to support your body weight on one knee and hand.

**Equipment variation:**

- Elastic resistance (Figure 62)

**Figure 62**
Triceps kickback; variation
using elastic resistance

a.            b.

# Biceps

**Muscles involved:** Biceps brachii, brachialis, brachioradialis, pronator teres

**Strength-training technique for the biceps:**

> Participants may overgrip weights or elastic resistance, which fatigues the forearm isometrically and can elevate blood pressure.

**Table 6**
**Exercises for the biceps**

**weights**

| position | exercise | variation | equipment |
|---|---|---|---|
| standing | biceps curls | single arm, reverse curls, hammer curls | bars |

**elastic resistance**

| position | exercise | variations | equipment |
|---|---|---|---|
| standing | biceps curls | single arm | |
| floor | seated curls | | bench |
| | decline curls | | bench |

*Biceps Curl*

**Targeted muscle:** Biceps

**Starting position:** Stand erect with your knees slightly bent and contract the transverse abdominis to help maintain neutral spine. Arms hang down along the sides of the body with the palms facing forward (Figure 63).

**Action:** Simultaneously curl both dumbbells up to shoulder height, pause, and slowly lower arms to the starting position (Figure 64).

**Common errors:**

*Error:* Swinging arms or elbows

*Correction:* Stabilize your elbows directly under the shoulders and next to the torso throughout the movement.

*Error:* Overgripping the weight

*Correction:* Gently grasp the weight so there is no chance of dropping it.

**Figure 63**
Biceps curl; starting position

**Variations:**

- Seated on the narrow end of bench
- One arm at a time
- Begin with the palm facing the side of the body and supinate the lower arm during the lift.
- Begin with the palm facing the side of the body and maintain that position throughout the exercise.

**Figure 64**
Biceps curl; action

# Torso

**Muscles involved:** Rectus abdominis, internal obliques, external obliques, erector spinae

**Strength-training techniques for the torso:**

1. Keep the knees slightly bent to maintain neutral spinal alignment. This allows the pelvis to have greater mobility to adjust into a supportive position.

2. To work the whole range of the abdominals, participants need to move the pelvis (usually by performing a pelvic tilt) as well as the rib cage.

3. If the hip flexors are too involved in the exercise, create a hamstring contraction by digging in the heels. In so doing, the antagonist muscle group, the hip flexors, will relax.

4. Avoid flapping the arms, pulling on the neck, and other movements that decrease the workload on the abdominal muscles.

5. You can perform high numbers of repetitions of abdominal exercises in multiple sets on non-consecutive days.

6. Torso exercises can be modified by extending one or both arms to increase the lever length of the body.

7. Make sure stability balls are firmly in place to ensure safety and effectiveness.

**Table 7**
**Exercises for the torso**

| bodyweight | | | |
|---|---|---|---|
| *position* | *exercise* | *variation* | *equipment* |
| floor | abdominal curls | decline bench | weights, ball |
| | oblique curls | | weights, balls |
| | pelvic tilt | seated | balls |
| | prone trunk hyperextension | | bench balls |
| | prone alternating arm and leg raises | | exercise balls |

*Abdominal Curl*

**Targeted muscle:** Rectus abdominis

**Starting position:** Lie supine with knees bent and feet flat on the floor, shoulder-width apart. Cross your arms over your chest or place them, unclasped, behind the head with the elbows out to the side. Maintain neutral alignment in the cervical spine (Figure 65).

**Action:** Contract the abdominals and exhale as you curl up. Lead with the rib cage and raise your shoulders and upper back off the floor toward the pelvis. Contract at the top of the movement, pause, then slowly return to the starting position (Figure 66).

**Figure 65**
Abdominal curl; starting position

**Figure 66**
Abdominal curl; action

**Common errors:**

*Error:* Forward neck position

*Correction:* Imagine an apple tucked between your chin and neck and maintain this position throughout the exercise.

*Error:* Moving arms

*Correction:* Keep your elbows out of vision.

*Error:* Holding the breath

*Correction:* Emphasize exhaling during the exertion phase.

**Variations:**

- Leg positions; changing the angle of the hips or knees
- Changing arm position and lever length to increase or decrease intensity

**Equipment variations:**

- Dumbbells; hold a weight on the chest
- Decline with bench (advanced)
- Feet up on a bench

*Oblique Curl*

**Targeted muscle:** External and internal obliques

**Starting position:** Lie supine with knees bent and feet flat on floor, shoulder-width apart. Cross your left ankle over your right knee. Place hands at the sides of the head (unclasped) with your elbows out to the side (Figure 67).

**Action:** Contract the transverse abdominis as you rotate up, keeping the head, neck, and shoulder blades in alignment. Lead with the rib cage and cross the right shoulder to the left knee. Contract at the top of the motion and slowly return to starting position (Figure 68). Repeat to the other side.

**Figure 67**
Oblique curl;
starting
position

**Figure 68**
Oblique curl;
action

**Common errors:**

*Error:* Forward neck position

*Correction:* Imagine an apple tucked between your chin and neck and maintain this position throughout the exercise.

*Error:* Moving arms

*Correction:* Keep your elbows out of vision.

*Error:* Holding the breath

*Correction:* Emphasize exhaling during the exertion phase.

**Variations:**

- Leg positions; changing the angle of the hips or knees
- Changing arm position and lever length to increase or decrease intensity

**Equipment variations:**

- Dumbbells; hold a weight behind the head or on the chest
- Decline with bench (advanced)
- Feet up on a bench

*Reverse Curl*

**Targeted muscle:** Rectus abdominis

**Starting position:** Lie supine with hips flexed 90 degrees or more. Extend arms flat at your sides and maintain neutral alignment in the cervical spine (Figure 69).

**Action:** Lift your knees and legs in an upward diagonal direction over the belly button, pause, then slowly lower the legs to the starting position (Figure 70).

**Figure 69**
Reverse curl; starting position

**Common errors:**

*Error:* Using hands or arms as leverage

*Correction:* Relax the arms, cross the arms over the chest, or turn the palms up.

*Error:* Holding the breath

*Correction:* Emphasize exhaling during the exertion phase.

**Figure 70**
Reverse curl; action

**Variations:**

- Leg positions: changing the angle of the hips or knees
- One hip flexed 90 degrees while the other leg is bent at the knee with the foot flat on the floor for support (Figure 71)

**Equipment variations:**

- Inline with bench (advanced)
- Feet up on a bench

**Figure 71**
Reverse curl; variation

*Prone Back Extension*

**Targeted muscle:** Erector spinae

**Starting position:** Begin by lying prone with your hips pressed into the floor and abdominal muscles contracted to stabilize the spine and pelvis (Figure 72).

**Action:** Lift the left arm and the right leg simultaneously, pause, then slowly return to the starting position (Figure 73). Repeat on opposite side.

**Figure 72**
Prone back extension; starting position

**Figure 73**
Prone back extension; action

**Common errors:**

*Error:* Holding the breath

*Correction:* Emphasize exhaling during the lifting phase of the exercise.

*Error:* Excessive extension of the lumbar and cervical spine

*Correction:* Control the lifting phase and limit the range of motion of the neck and lower back, keeping your neck in alignment with the spine.

**Variations:**

- On hands on knees
- Only upper body
- Lift both arms and both legs simultaneously
- Change arm position and lever length to increase or decrease intensity

**Equipment variations:**

- Exercise ball (Figure 74)
- Decline on bench

**Figure 74**
Prone back extension; variation using exercise ball

# Upper Legs and Hips

**Muscles involved:** Quadriceps, hamstrings, hip abductors, hip adductors, gluteus maximus, hip flexors

**Strength-training techniques for the upper leg:**

1. When using elastic resistance, placing the band above the knee creates less stress than placing the band below the knee.

2. Always keep the knee from gliding past the position directly over the ankles.

3. Stepping backward into a lunge places less stress on the knee than stepping forward into a lunge.

4. When strengthening the hips, contract the transverse abdominis and keep the spine neutral.

**Table 8**
**Exercises for the upper legs and hips**

**bodyweight, weights**
**elastic resistance**

| position | exercise | variation | equipment |
|----------|----------|-----------|-----------|
| standing | squats | | dumbbells, elastic resistance, bodybars |
| | backward lunges | front and side | dumbbells, elastic resistance, bodybars |
| floor | quadriceps extension | | bench, elastic resistance |
| | hamstrings curl | | bench, elastic resistance |
| | straight leg extensions | | bench, elastic resistance |
| | outer thigh lift | | elastic resistance, body bar |
| | inner thigh lift | | elastic resistance, body bar |

*Squat*

**Targeted muscle:** Gluteals, hamstrings, quadriceps

**Starting position:** Stand erect with a neutral spine and feet shoulder-width apart (Figure 75).

**Action:** Slowly lower the body, with the hips moving back as if sitting in a chair. Maintain the weight directly over the heels or mid-foot. Lower to approximately 90 degrees of knee flexion, pause, then slowly return to the starting position (Figure 76). If lumbar curvature cannot be maintained, lower less than 90 degrees.

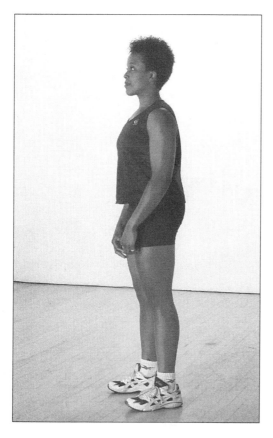

**Figure 75**
Squat; starting position

**Common errors:**

*Error:* Lowering beyond 90 degrees flexion

*Correction:* Slowly lower the body and stop before the upper leg becomes parallel with the floor.

*Error:* Forward lean with heel lift

*Correction:* Keep your weight over the back portion of the foot rather than the toes; raise your arms to shoulder height to counterbalance.

**Variation:**

- One leg at a time

**Equipment variation:**

- Elastic resistance secured onto straight bar (Figure 77)

**Figure 76**
Squat;
action

**Figure 77**
Squat; variation using elastic resistance secured onto a straight bar

a.

b.

*Backward Lunges*

**Targeted muscles:** Gluteals, hamstrings, quadriceps

**Starting position:** Stand erect with a neutral spine and feet shoulder-width apart (Figure 78).

**Action:** Take a long step backward landing on the ball of the foot and bend the rear knee to a fencer's lunge position; lower to approximately 90 degrees of knee flexion (Figure 79). Pause, then push back to standing position. Maintain neutral spine throughout the movement.

**Figure 78**
Backward lunge; starting position

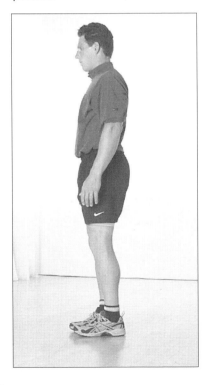

**Figure 79**
Backward lunge; action

**Common errors:**

*Error:* Dropping the head and shoulders forward

*Correction:* Keep your chest lifted over top of the hips and look straight ahead with neck in neutral position.

*Error:* Lowering beyond 90 degrees flexion

*Correction:* Slowly lower the body, and stop before the upper leg becomes parallel with the floor.

*Error:* Forward lean with heel lift of lead leg

*Correction:* Keep your weight over the back portion of the foot rather than the toes; raise your arms to shoulder height to counterbalance.

**Variations:**

- Side lunges (Figure 80)

**Figure 80**
Side lunge

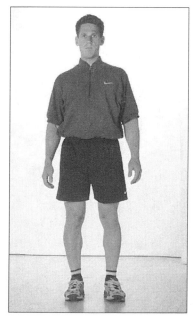

a.  b.

- Front lunges (Figure 81)
- Walking lunges

**Equipment variation:**

- Elastic resistance secured onto straight bar

**Figure 81**
Front lunge

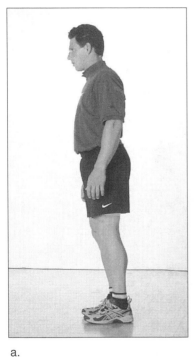

a.

b.

*Quadriceps Extension*

**Targeted muscle:** Quadriceps

**Starting position:** Sit with both legs bent at the knee and the feet flat on the floor. Secure a band around the working leg, which is bent 90 degrees (Figure 82).

**Action:** Slowly flex the knee until the leg is nearly straight, pause, then slowly return to starting position (Figure 83).

**Figure 82**
Quadriceps extension; starting position

**Common error:**

> *Error:* Leaning forward
>
> *Correction:* Keep your chest high and shoulders aligned with the hips.

**Variation:**

- Seated on bench

**Figure 83**
Quadriceps extension; action

*Hamstrings Curl*

**Targeted muscle:** Hamstrings

**Starting position:** Stand erect with a neutral spine and feet shoulder-width apart. Secure elastic resistance around the ankle of the working leg, which is slightly bent (Figure 84).

**Action:** Slowly flex the knee through a full range of motion, pause, then slowly return to starting position (Figure 85).

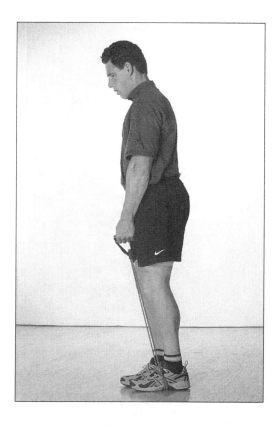

**Figure 84**
Hamstrings curl; starting position

**Common error:**

*Error:* Leaning forward

*Correction:* Keep the chest high and shoulders aligned with hips.

**Variation:**

- Prone on bench

**Figure 85**
Hamstrings curl; action

*Straight Leg Extensions*

**Targeted muscle:** Iliopsoas

**Starting position:** Sit with one leg bent and the other extended. Contract the transverse abdominis to help stabilize the spine and pelvis (Figure 86).

**Action:** Keep the leg extended and slowly raise the straight leg off the floor (Figure 87). Pause, then slowly return to starting position.

**Figure 86**
Straight leg extensions; starting position

**Variations:**

- Standing
- Bend the knee of the leg being lifted to decrease intensity by shortening the length of the lever.

**Equipment variations:**

- Dumbbells (leg weights) placed above the knee in the lying position
- Elastic resistance (standing or lying)

**Figure 87**
Straight leg extensions; action

*Outer Thigh Lift*

**Targeted muscle:** Gluteus medius, hip adductors

**Starting position:** Lie on your left side, and rest your head on your arm or hand. Bend your left leg and contract the transverse abdominis to help stabilize the spine and pelvis. Keep your right leg extended and toes pointed forward (Figure 88).

**Action:** Abduct the leg through a full range of motion, pause, then slowly return to the starting position (Figure 89). Repeat with other leg.

**Figure 88**
Outer thigh lift;
starting position

**Variations:**

- Standing
- Bend the knee of the leg being lifted to decrease intensity by shortening the length of the lever.

**Equipment variations:**

- Dumbbells (leg weights) placed above the knee in the lying position
- Elastic resistance (standing or lying)

**Figure 89**
Outer thigh lift; action

*Inner Thigh Lift*

**Targeted muscle:** Hip adductor

**Starting position:** Lie on your left side, and rest your head on your arm or hand. Hips and shoulders should face forward with transverse abdominis contracted to help stabilize the spine and pelvis. Straighten the bottom leg, then bend and cross your top leg over it (Figure 90).

**Action:** Slowly lift the bottom leg through a full range of motion, pause, then slowly return to the starting position (Figure 91). Repeat with the other leg.

**Figure 90**
Inner thigh lift; starting position

**Variations:**

- Bend the knee of the leg being lifted to decrease intensity by shortening the length of the lever.
- Supine; bend both legs 90 degrees and simultaneously adduct

**Equipment variations:**

- Dumbbells (leg weights) placed above the knee in the lying position
- Elastic resistance (standing or lying)

**Figure 91**
Inner thigh lift; action

# Lower Leg

**Muscles involved:** Plantar flexors, dorsiflexors

**Strength-training technique for the lower leg:**

During heel raises, especially on a step or bench, use the wall or body bar for extra stability.

**Table 9**
**Exercises for the lower leg**

| position | exercise | variation | equipment |
|---|---|---|---|
| **bodyweight** | | | |
| standing | heel raises | | bench step |
| **weights** | | | |
| position | exercise | variation | equipment |
| standing | heel raises | | bars, bench, step |

*Heel Raises*

**Targeted muscle:** Gastrocnemius, soleus

**Starting position:** Start with feet shoulder-width apart, knees slightly bent, and transverse abdominis contracted to help support the lower back (Figure 92).

**Action:** Raise up on toes, pause, then slowly lower to the starting position (Figure 93).

**Variation:**

- One foot at a time, hanging the heel of working leg off the edge of a bench while the other leg maintains full contact with the bench (Figure 94).

**Equipment variations:**

- Dumbbells held at waist or shoulder level
- Body bar held on top of shoulders

**Figure 92**
Heel raises;
starting
position

**Figure 93**
Heel raises;
action

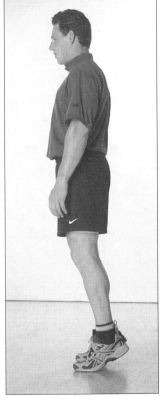

a.

**figure 94**
Heel raises;
variation using
a step

b.

*Toe Raises*

**Targeted muscle:** Anterior tibialis

**Starting position:** In a seated position, place one foot on top of the other (Figure 95).

**Figure 95**
Toe raises; starting position

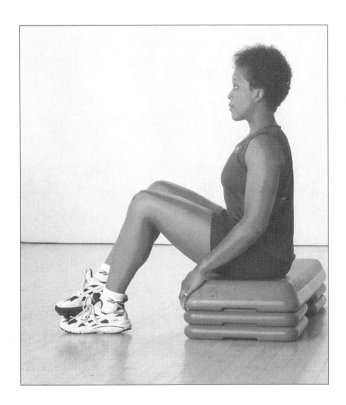

**Action:** Dorsiflex against the resistance applied by the non-working foot (Figure 96).

**Variation:**

- Rotate the foot inward and outward to work different aspects of the anterior shin.

**Equipment variation:**

- Place elastic resistance around middle of foot.

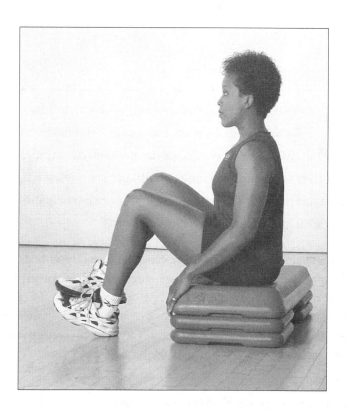

**Figure 96**
Toe raises;
action

# Chapter Four

# Teaching a Group Strength Training Class

## Verbal Introduction

Before beginning class, introduce yourself, the class or class format, and review some safety reminders relevant to the class. Encourage participants to communicate to you if they are feeling discomfort with any specific exercise or movement pattern. This should also prepare participants for the one-on-one feedback given during class.

> "Good morning. My name is Chris. Welcome to the Upper-body Design Class. Before we get started I wanted to remind you to go at your own pace throughout the class. We can always adjust the resistance, the exercise, or your alignment to make the exercise work for you. I will be circulating through the class so that I can provide you with feedback to keep you exercising effectively.
>
> Please do the following:
>
> If you feel any acute pain, stop and let me know.
>
> Drink plenty of water.
>
> Take breaks when necessary."

# Risk Assessment

On any given day, a new participant can enter a group fitness class and be a walking time bomb. The participant can have advanced coronary disease, **arthritis**, or severe low back pain. When placed in a group situation, the participant may not disclose his or her medical history to you. Moreover, a regular participant may develop a condition that poses new challenges to completing a strength-training class.

For these reasons, it is vitally important to screen participants during the introduction before class starts. Some participant may even require a medical screening prior to exercising.

Speak to new participants individually. Exchange simple information, such as names and commonalities. Ask the individual if he or she has any medical concerns, medications, or muscloskeletal challenges that needs to be discussed. Also, ask if participants have any changes in their health status that need to be addressed. If the participant has not already completed informed consent and health history forms, have them do so for your records.

# Technique Review

Proper exercise execution can only occur if participants are in the proper starting position. A simple method for guiding participants into proper alignment is using either a toe-to-head or head-to-toe approach. Using this method, you can ensure that the key areas of the body are guided into proper alignment. As cues are given, begin at one end of the body and work toward the other end of the body. Following are examples of guiding participants into abdominal curls using the two different methods. Note that the cues are the same, but the order is different.

*Head-to-toe* – Support your head with the palms of your hands, elbows to the side, neutral spine, knees and feet shoulder-width apart.

*Toe-to-head* – Feet and knees shoulder-width apart, neutral spine, support your head with the palms of your hands, and elbows to the side.

# Cueing

**C**ueing helps participants understand how the exercise should be performed as well as what to do next. There are three different categories of cues offered during class.

1. Movement cues initiate movements and/or modify existing movements.

   *For example:* "three up and one down; single arm only; front then side"

2. Motivational cues help increase the motivation and effort of the participants

   *For example:* "squeeze," "getting stronger," or "almost done"

3. Safety and alignment cues help improve the performance of the exercise.

   *For example:* "keep your knee over your ankle" or "support your lower back by placing one hand on your mid-thigh"

## Types of Feedback

There are four components to a complete feedback statement. Use them individually or in sequence.

### Knowledge of Results

This type of feedback is a nonjudgmental statement that simply informs the participant of what you are observing. Some examples of knowledge of results feedback are:

"Your face is bright red."

"Your knee is over your toes."

"Your lower back is arched excessively."

The purpose of this type of feedback is to act like a mirror. Describe the performance, good or bad, of the participant. Ultimately, participants must learn to recognize when they are performing the movement incorrectly.

### Corrective

This type of feedback states the correct method of performance. It lets participants know the specific performance that is required. Some examples of corrective feedback are:

"Exhale during the exertion."

"Move your knee above your ankle."

"Keep the spine neutral."

This type of feedback may also include statements that can help the participants learn to regulate their own performance. For example, explain that when the knee moves forward over the foot it blocks the view of the shoelaces. In this way, the participant can begin to self-regulate performance.

### Confirming

This type of feedback lets participants know when they have performed the movement correctly. Some examples of this type of feedback are:

"That's the way!"

"You got it!"

"That's right!"

### Instructional

This type of feedback offers an explanation or rationale behind the feedback. Participants can fully understand the importance and consequences of their performances. With greater understanding of the rationale, compliance and motivation will increase. For example, explain that holding the breath during strength-training exercises can elevate blood pressure. Therefore, an established breathing pattern can reduce an elevation in blood pressure.

## Feedback Statements

There are three types of strategies for giving feedback statements during class.

1. The overhead statement is not directed at any one person and is offered to the entire class. This is useful when you see incorrect form in more than one participant and do not want to draw attention to any single individual.

2. The proximal statement is made for the benefit of all participants but with one or two individuals in mind. Move close to the participant or participants that require feedback. Do not directly face the participant, but place yourself in the participant's personal space; it is most effective when you are in the direct line of view of the participant.

3. The direct statement is made directly to the participant who requires feedback. Although some participants may feel awkward with this approach, it is necessary to ensure the exercises are performed safely and effectively.

# Intensity Monitoring

Make every effort to walk around the entire room. Besides the benefit of giving each person an acknowledgment, this gives you an opportunity to monitor intensity and performance.

It has been shown that when a participant holds his breath during strenuous exercise there is an increased elevation in blood pressure. Although most instructors urge participants to exhale during the lifting phase of an exercise, a relaxed breathing pattern during the lowering phase is equally effective.

Monitor each participant to ensure that he is not holding the breath. A red or strenuous look on a participant's face may be an indication that he needs to breath more regularly.

## To Touch or Not to Touch

One-on-one training can occur in a group setting. As you move around the room monitoring participants, one-on-one instruction inevitably takes place. Use discretion and always ask permission prior to touching any participants. A simple question, "May I touch your shoulder to help teach you the movement?" will let you know how comfortable the participant is with touching.

The value of using touch is tremendous and is a highly effective teaching tool. There are two strategies you can use: the "hands-on" method and the "hands-off" method.

**Example #1:** You are leading a single arm triceps kickback using weights and notice that a participant's elbow drops during the movement rather than remaining stationary.

*Hands-on:* Place your palm or the back of your hand in the correct spot for the elbow. Instruct the participant to keep contact with the elbow on the hand for the entire range of motion. When the elbow drifts off the hand, the participant feels the change and begins to become more aware of the error.

*Hands-off:* Place the participant's elbow in the correct starting position, then place your own hand about one inch underneath the participant's upper arm near the elbow, but without touching it. When the participant's elbow drops, they feel your hand, which helps them become more aware of the error.

**Example #2:** A participant is performing a front deltoid raise. You notice that she is raising her arms too high.

*Hands-on:* Place your hand at the correct spot for the top of the movement. The participant raises her arms up until they touch your hands, and begins to become aware of how the movement feels when performed correctly.

*Hands-off:* Place your hand slightly above the top of the movement. When the participant raises her arms too high, she touches your hand, and begins to become aware of how the movement feels when performed correctly.

# Injury Prevention

To avoid injury to the spine and back muscles, teach participants to maintain a neutral spinal alignment, which is the position in which the spine is best equipped to deal with external stress and strain. Unlike other exercises that are specific to the classroom, postural maintenance is performed throughout the day.

Table 10
**Postural deviations and associated muscle imbalances**

| Malalignment | Possible Tight Muscles | Possible Weak Muscles |
|---|---|---|
| Excessive lordosis | Lower back (erectors), hip flexors | Abdominals (especially obliques, lower fibers of rectus abdominis), hip extensors |
| Flat-back | Upper abdominals, hip extensors | Lower back (erectors), hip flexors |
| Sway-back | Upper abdominals, hip flexors | Obliques, lower rectus abdominis, hip extensors |
| Excessive kyphosis | Upper abdominals, internal obliques, shoulder adductors, internal rotators (pectorals and latissimus), intercostals | Erector spinae of the thoracic spine, scapular adductors (mid and lower trapezius) |
| Forward neck | Cervical flexors, upper trapezius | Neck extensors |

When teaching in a room with mirrors, have participants view their spinal alignment from the side so they can become more aware of their alignment.

It is estimated that close to 80% of the population will suffer an episode of lower-back pain. Therefore, avoid placing excessive stress on the lower back and be aware if any of your participants have a history of lower-back pain.

### Establishing Range of Motion Limits

Some exercises have established range of motion (ROM) limits, or stopping points. Movement that goes beyond this point can cause injury. Identify these ROM limits prior to starting the exercise. In this way, participants can increase their awareness of the crucial position.

For example, during the supine chest fly exercise, it is common for participants to lower the arms too fast, which causes the arms to drop too low. Remedy this by establishing the lower range of motion as the starting point. Lifting up from the starting point and then emphasizing the slow and controlled lowering of the arms can help avoid moving beyond the safe limits of the exercise.

# Modifications

There are three ways to modify strength-training intensity: external resistance, lever changes (modifying the body position to work against gravity), and active rest.

### External Resistance

To increase the intensity, increase the resistance (e.g., increase the weight, shorten the band, choose a band with greater resistance, or add manual resistance). To decrease the intensity, reduce the resistance (e.g., reduce the weight, lengthen the band, or choose a band with less resistance).

### Lever Changes

To decrease intensity, shorten the lever by bending the elbows or placing the weight closer to the joint that is moving. To increase intensity, lengthen the lever or move the weight further from the joint that is moving.

### Active Rest

To increase the intensity, decrease the amount of rest between sets or between repetitions. To decrease intensity, perform fewer repetitions by alternating between right and left sides or by alternating between lifting and resting.

For example, lateral deltoid raises can be modified to reduce the intensity in the following ways:

1. Reduce the weight being lifted.
2. Bend the elbow 90 degrees.
3. Alternate between right and left sides or between lateral raises and biceps curls.

In addition to intensity modifications, you may need to offer modifications to reduce the stress on the lower back.

Overhead exercises can be performed with one arm at a time to reduce the stress on the spine. Bent-over and standing exercises can be modified into a staggered stance with one leg forward and one leg backward. The hand that is on the same side as the forward leg is placed on the upper thigh for support. This leaves the other hand free for single arm exercises.

On the floor, extended legs can decrease the mobility of the pelvis and encourage poor posture. Bend the knees and bring the feet closer to the hips in order to support the back.

# Chapter Five

# Programming

## Warm-up

Each strength-training class should begin with a gradual warm-up to psychologically and physically prepare participants for the workout. The focus of the warm-up should be on joint preparation and rehearsal of movements to be used in class.

## Cool-down

Because blood tends to accumulate in the lower body when vigorous exercise is stopped abruptly, lower-intensity exercises are recommended to help actively recover. As a general guideline, the last five to 10 minutes of the class should be dedicated to cool-down activity.

Always make sure that participants have fully recovered and are below 60% of maximum heart rate before transitioning to a floor position. Quickly moving from a standing to lying position causes pooled blood to rush toward the heart. Participants with compromised cardiovascular systems should be particularly cautious as this can lead to heart attacks or other failures of the cardiovascular system.

# Exercise Sequencing

There are three formats used to sequence exercises into a class: 1) upper/lower, 2) large to small, and 3) agonist/antagonist.

## Upper/Lower

In this format, alternate between upper- and lower-body exercises, allowing for ample recovery time for each body part.

*Sample class*

**Start standing with elastic resistance:**

Chest press / Squats / One arm row / Backward lunges

**Standing with weights:**

Side lateral raises / Side leg lifts with the weight slightly proximal to the knee / Triceps kickbacks / Side lunges / Biceps curl / Calf raises

**On the floor with elastic resistance:**

Push ups / Prone leg curls / Seated low rows / Seated leg extensions / Seated biceps curl / Seated hip flexion

**On the floor with weights:**

Supine triceps extension / Hip abduction / One arm triceps push ups / Hip adduction

**Abdominals followed by slow stretching:**

Curl up / Supine full-body stretch with arms reaching overhead

Each pair can be a performed as a single set or in a two-set format.

## Large to Small

This format begins with large muscle groups of the legs and works progressively toward the smaller muscle groups of the torso and arms. Participants work the larger muscle groups when they are least fatigued.

Plan transitions so starting positions (standing vs. floor) and equipment variations (weights vs. elastic resistance) are closely related. Avoid changing both starting position and equipment in succession.

| **Exercise** | **(Transitions)** |
|---|---|
| *5–10 minute warm up* | |
| *Quadriceps, Hamstrings, Gluteals* – Squats, walking lunges | (Begin standing) |
| *Hamstrings* – Hamstring curl with elastic resistance | (Equipment) |
| *Abductors* – Floor abduction with elastic resistance | (Starting position) |
| *Adductors* – Floor Adductors with exercise ball | (Equipment) |
| *Abdominals* – Curl up or oblique curl up | (Equipment) |
| *Back extensors* – Prone; alternating arm and leg raise | (None) |
| *Chest* – Push ups | (None) |
| *Back* – Seated row with elastic resistance | (Equipment) |
| *Shoulders* – Standing lateral deltoid raise | (Starting position) |
| *Shoulders* – Standing overhead press with weights | (Equipment) |
| *Biceps* – Bicep curls with weights | (None) |
| *Triceps* – Seated tricep overhead press | (Starting position) |
| *Slow stretching* | (None) |

Each pair can be a performed as a single set or in a two-set format.

## Agonist/Antagonist

This format works opposing muscle groups in pairs. This helps prevent muscle imbalances caused by strengthening only one muscle group.

### Chest / Back
*Weights:* Supine chest fly / One arm row on bench
*Elastic resistance:* Standing chest press / Single arm lat pull down

### Shoulders
*Weights:* Front deltoid raise / Posterior shoulder extension
*Elastic resistance:* Arnold press / Posterior shoulder extension

### Biceps / Triceps
*Weights:* Biceps curl / Tricep kickback
*Elastic resistance:* Seated bicep curls / Overhead tricep press

### Torso
Abdominal curls / Prone trunk hyperextension

### Quadriceps / Hamstrings
*Leg weights:* Knee to chest / Leg curls

### Hip abductors / Hip adductors
*Weights:* Standing abduction / Squats with ball squeezed between knees
*Elastic resistance:* Abduction / Adduction

### Plantar flexors / Dorsiflexors
Heel raises / Toe raises

Each pair can be a performed as a single set or in a two-set format.

# Group Circuit Class

A circuit class provides cardiovascular-endurance training along with muscular-endurance training. The circuit can be modified to meet the fitness level of the participants as well as space, equipment, and time limitations.

*Sample Class: Combo Circuit Class*

*Fitness level:* Moderate to advanced

*Time:* 45 minutes (set-up and break-down time is not included)

*Music tempo:* 120–130 bpm

*Class size:* Provide one piece of equipment per station for each group of 15 participants. A class size of 16–30 participants requires two pieces of equipment at each station.

Equipment: Station equipment, stop watch, whistle, towel (to clean sweat on equipment or on floor), and treats for the end of class (e.g., orange slices, apples, etc.).

**Directions:** Set up 15 stations around the room (Figure 97). Place a sign at each station that indicates the name and number of the exercise within the sequence. For example, the sign for the first station would display "#1-Push-up."

After a five-minute warm-up, have each participant move to a station. Provide beginners with a buddy who can help them work through the circuit and place them at station #1 to make the circuit easier to understand.

For the first minute, each participant performs a station exercise. Using the stop watch, indicate the 30 second mark and the 50 second mark (10 seconds left.) You can also prepare a tape recording that alternates between 60 seconds of music and 20–30 seconds of silence to indicate transition time between stations.

**Figure 97**
Group Circuit Class

| Station # | Exercise | Equipment |
|---|---|---|
| 1 | push ups | exercise mat |
| 2 | sit ups | exercise mat |
| 3 | pull ups | pull up bar in doorway / exercise band |
| 4 | oblique crunches | exercise mat |
| 5 | front deltoid raises | dumbbell or bands |
| 6 | bouncing | mini-trampoline |
| 7 | side deltoid raise | dumbbell or exercise band |
| 8 | jump rope | jump rope |
| 9 | bicep curl | dumbbell or exercise band |
| 10 | jumping jacks | |
| 11 | tricep curls | dumbbell or exercise band |
| 12 | step (over the top*) | step or bench |
| 13 | squats | dumbbell or exercise band |
| 14 | towel jump | towel or a line of masking tape on floor |
| 15 | walking lunges | dumbbell |

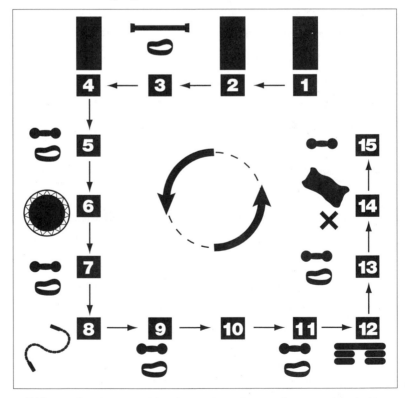

*When performing step training, choose alternating exercises to work both sides of the body, or exercise 30 seconds on one leg and 30 seconds on the other.

Blow the whistle to signal the movement of the class to the next station in the circuit. After 15 minutes, each station has been performed once. After 30 minutes, or two complete cycles, begin the cool-down. A five-minute cool-down followed by five minutes of stretching allows for proper recovery.

*Variations:* Use cardio equipment, bikes, rowing machines, or trampolines. Add sports-specific exercises (e.g., power leaps and hops). Add a 15–30 second transition exercise, such as jumping jacks or shuffle exercises, in between the stations.

## Music

Select music to make the class fun and enjoyable for all participants. To ensure the exercises are performed slowly and with control, the music's **beats** per minute (bpm) should fall within the range of 110–130 bpm. When the tempo of the music is faster than 130 bpm, there is a tendency for alignment and form to decline. This is especially true for beginning participants. Music that is extremely fast, above 180 bpm, can be performed at half time (i.e., moving to every other beat of the music) in order to compensate.

Because music influences the way people perform the exercises, it is also recommended that the concentric muscle action is placed with the downbeat, or on the "1 count." For example, when abdominal curls are done so the eccentric muscle action is placed with the downbeat, participants tend to accelerate through the eccentric phase rather than controlling the movement. In this particular case, participants appear to throw their head down toward the floor and then lift up to starting position rather than lifting smoothly through the movement.

# Glossary

**Agonist** – A muscle that is directly engaged in contraction; opposes the action of an antagonist muscle.

**Antagonist** – A muscle that acts in opposition to the action produced by an agonist.

**Applied Force** – An external force acting on a system (body or body segment).

**Arthritis** – Inflammatory condition involving a joint.

**Beats** – Regular pulsations that have an even rhythm and occur in a continuous pattern of strong and weak pulsations.

**Body Composition** – The makeup of the body in terms of percentage of lean body mass and body fat.

**Bursitis** – Irritation of a bursa, which is a padlike fluid-filled sac located at friction sites throughout the body; bursitis occurs most often in the knees, hips, shoulders, and elbows.

**Calisthenics** – Exercises to increase muscular strength or endurance that use the weight of the body or body parts for resistance.

**Chondromalacia** – A gradual softening and degeneration of the articular cartilage, usually involving the back surface of the patella (knee cap). This condition may produce pain and swelling, or a grinding sound or sensation when the knee is flexed and extended.

**Concentric** – A muscle action in which the muscle shortens.

**Contraindication** – Any condition that renders some particular movement, activity, or treatment improper or undesirable.

**Cueing** – A visual or verbal technique, using hand signals or only a few words, to inform exercise participants of upcoming movements.

**Eccentric** – A muscle action in which the muscle lengthens against a resistance while producing force.

**Extension** – Movement that increases the angle between two bones of a joint, such as straightening of the elbow.

**Flexion** – The movement that decreases the angle between two bones of a joint.

**Force Arm** – The lever arm length (the perpendicular distance from the axis to the line of the force) of the motive force.

**Isometric** – Muscular contraction in which there is no change in the angle of the involved joint(s) and little or no change in the length of the contracting muscle.

**Kinesiology** – The study of the principles of mechanics and anatomy in relation to human movement.

**Lever** – A rigid bar that rotates around a fixed support (fulcrum) in response to an applied force.

**Low Back Pain (LBP)** - A general term to describe a multitude of back conditions, including muscular and ligament strains, sprains, and injuries. The cause of LBP is often elusive; most LBP is probably caused by muscle imbalance and weakness.

**Muscular Endurance** – The ability of a muscle or muscle group to exert force against a resistance over a sustained period of time.

**Muscular Strength** – The maximal force a muscle or muscle group can exert during a single contraction.

**Strength Training** – The process of exercising with progressively heavier resistance for the purpose of strengthening the musculoskeletal system.

# Index

## A

abdominal curls, 72, 73-74
activities of daily living, 4
agonist, 120
agonist/antagonist exercise
   sequencing, 116
antagonist, 120
anterior deltoids, 20, 24, 27,
   44, 46
anterior shoulder, 20
anterior tibialis, 102
applied force, 120
Arnold press, 45, 51
arthritis, 105, 120

## B

back exercises, 30
   bent over row, 31, 32-33
   scapular adduction, 40-43
   seated row, 42-44
   shrugs, 34-35
   upright row, 36-37
backward lunges, 82, 86-88
bands, 13, 14-15
beats per minute (bpm), 119, 120
bench dips, 59-62
bench push ups, 23
benches, 13
bent over row, 31, 32-33
   single arm variation, 33
biceps, 69-71
biceps brachii, 59, 69
biceps curls, 69-71
bikes, 119
body bars, 13

body composition, 120
body weight, reducing of, 4
bone strength, 5
brachialis, 59, 69
brachioradialis, 59, 69
breathing pattern, 108-109
buddy, 117
bursitis, 120

## C

calisthenics, 3, 120
cardiovascular-endurance
   training, 117
chest exercises, 20
   chest press, 27-30
   push ups, 20-24
   strength-training
     techniques, 20
   supine chest fly, 14, 24-26
chondromalacia, 120
circuit class, 117-119
combo circuit class, 117-119
concentric, 120
concentric muscle action, 12,
   16, 119
constant vs. variable exercise
   equipment, 13-14
contractions, types of, 11-13
contraindication, 120
cool-down, 113-114, 119
coronary disease, 105
corrective feedback, 107
cueing, 106-108, 120
curls
   abdominal, 72, 73-74
   biceps, 69-71

decline, 69
hammer, 69
hamstring, 82, 91-92
oblique, 72, 75-76
reverse, 77-79
standing biceps, 8-10, 11

# D

decline curls, 69
deep knee flexion, 3
deltoids
    anterior, 20, 24, 27, 44, 46
    middle, 36, 44, 48, 50
    posterior, 44, 52
direct statement, 108
dorsiflexors, 99
downbeat, 119
dumbbells, 13-15
    standing biceps curls with,
      8-10
    standing chest fly with, 7-8, 9
dynamic constant and variable
    resistance equipment, 13-15

# E

eccentric, 121
eccentric muscle action, 12,
    16, 119
elastic band, securing to feet,
    13, 44
elastic properties, 13
elastic resistance variations,
    8, 15
    bent over row, 33
    chest press, 28, 29
    push up, 22, 24
    shrugs, 35
    single arm lat pull-down,
      38, 39
    squat, 85

supine chest fly, 26
triceps kickback, 68
upper leg, 82
upright row, 37
equipment, 13-15
equipment variations, 115
erector spinae, 72, 80
excessive kyphosis, 110
excessive lordosis, 110
exercise analysis, 12
exercise balls, 13
    prone back extension, 81
    push up, 23
exercise frequency, 18
exercise mats, 13, 14
exercise progression, 17-18
exercise props, 13
exercise range, 16
exercise resistance, 16
exercise selection, 15
exercise sequencing, 15-16,
    114-117
exercise sets, 16
exercise speed, 16
extension, 7, 45, 121
external obliques, 72
external resistance, 111
eye contact, 3

# F

feedback, 2
    types of, 106-108
flat-back, 110
flexion, 3, 59, 121
force arm, 121
forward flexion, 3
forward neck, 110
frequency, of exercise, 18
front deltoid raises, 45, 46-47
front lunges, 88
functional exercises, 3

## G

gastrocnemius, 99
gluteals, 83, 86
gluteus maximus, 82
gluteus medius, 95
grip, 20, 30
group circuit class, 117-119
group strength training
    benefits, 4-5
    guidelines, 1-3
    history, 3-4

## H

hammer curls, 69
hamstring contraction, 72
hamstring curls, 82, 91-92
hamstrings, 82, 83, 86
hands-off and hands-on
    teaching, 109, 110
head-to-toe review, 106
health history form, 105
heel raises, 99-102
hip abductors, 82
hip adductors, 96, 97
hip flexors, 72, 82
hops, 119
hyperextension, 72

## I

iliopsoas, 93
informed consent, 105
infraspinatus, 55
injury prevention, 4, 110-111
inner thigh lift, 82, 97-98
instructional feedback, 107-108
instructions, 2
intensity, 17, 111
    modifications, 111-112

monitoring, 108-110
internal obliques, 72
internal shoulder rotation, 58
inward rotation, 55
isometric contraction, 11-12, 121

## J

joint flexibility, 16
joints, stress on, 15
jumping jacks, 119

## K

kinesiology, 6-18, 121
knowledge of results, 106-107
kyphosis, excessive, 110

## L

large to small exercise
    sequencing, 114-115
lat pull-down exercises, 30
lateral deltoid raises, 45, 48-49
    modification, 112
latissimus dorsi, 30, 38
levator scapula, 30
lever, 121
lever changes, 112
ligament tensile strength, 5
line of gravity, 7-10, 13
lordosis, excessive, 110
lower back pain (LBP), 30, 105,
    111, 121
lower back, stress on, 112
lower leg, 99-103
    heel raises, 99-102
    strength-training technique
      for, 99
    toe raises, 102-103
lunges, 82, 86-88

## M

mats, 13, 14
medical screening, 105
metabolic functioning,
    improvement of, 4
middle deltoid, 36, 44, 48, 50
mirrors, 111
modifications, 1-3, 10, 111-112
motivation, 4
motivational cues, 106
movement cues, 106
multiple sets, 16
muscle balance, 15
muscle contractile strength, 5
muscle fiber size, 5
muscle imbalance, 110
muscular endurance, 2, 121
music, 119

## N

neck position, 76
neutral neck position, 19
neutral spinal alignment, 19,
    44, 59, 72, 86, 110-111

## O

oblique curls, 72, 75-76
obliques, 75
one arm row, 31
one arm tricep push ups, 59
one-on-one training, 109
outer thigh lift, 82, 95-96
outward/external shoulder
    rotation, 55, 56-58
overhead press, 45, 50-52
overhead shoulder press, 44
overhead statement, 108
overhead triceps press, 15, 59,
    64-65

## P

pectoralis major, 20, 24, 27
pelvic tilt, 72
physical appearance,
    improvement of, 4
physical capacity, improvement
    of, 4
plantar flexors, 99
posterior deltoids, 44, 52
posterior shoulder, 45
posterior shoulder extension,
    52-54
power leaps, 119
programming
    cool-down, 113-114
    exercise sequencing, 114-117
    warm-up, 113
progression, of exercise, 17
pronator teres, 59
prone alternating arm and leg
    raises, 72
prone back extension, 80-81
prone trunk, 72
proper alignment, guiding,
    105-106
proximal statement, 108
push ups, 3, 14, 20-24
    bench, 23
    tricep, 62-64
    wall, 22

## Q

quadriceps, 82, 83, 86
quadriceps extension, 82, 89-90

## R

range of motion (ROM), 16
    limits of, 111
rectus abdominis, 72, 73, 77

# References and Suggested Reading

Brooks, D. (1993). *Theory and Mechanics of Resistance Training,* Mammoth Lakes, Calif.: Moves International.

Clarke, D.H. (1975). *Exercise Physiology,* Englewood Cliffs, N.J.: Prentice Hall Inc.

Crisco, J. & Panjabi, M.M. (1991). The intersegmental and multisegmental muscles of the lumbar spine. *Spine,* 16, 793–799.

Ellison, D. (1995). Exercise for function, part one. *IDEA Today,* March, 13, 3.

Ellison, D. (1995). Exercise for function, part two. *IDEA Today,* April, 13, 4.

Hall, T., David, A., Geere, J., & Salvenson, K. (1995). *Relative recruitment of the abdominal muscles during three levels of exertion during abdominal hollowing.* Gold Coast, Queensland: Manipulative Physiotherapists Association of Australia.

Hedrick, A. (1995). Training for hypertrophy. *Strength and Conditioning,* 17, 2, 22–29.

Hodges, P.W. & Richardson, C.A. (1995) Neuromotor dysfunction of the trunk musculature in low back pain patients. In: *Proceedings of the International Congress of the World Confederation of Physical Therapists.* Washington, D.C.

Hodges, P.W. & Richardson, C.A. (1996). Inefficient muscular stabilization of the lumbar spine associated with low back pain. *Spine,* 21, 22, 2640–2650.

Hodges, P.W., Richardson, C.A., & Jull, G. (1996). Evaluation of the relationship between laboratory and clinical tests of transverse abdominis function. *Physiotherapy Research International,* 1, 30–40.

Lacourse, M.G. (1994) Touching for strength. *IDEA Today,* May, 12, 5.

Richardson, C.A, Jull, G., Hodges, P.W., & Hides, J.A. (1999). *Therapeutic Exercise for Spinal Segmental Stabilization in Low Back Pain.* New York: Churchill Livingstone.

Wescott, W. (1994). *Strength Fitness* (4th ed.). Dubuque, Iowa: WCB/McGraw-Hill.

Wlodkowski, R.J. (1993) *Enhancing Adult Motivation to Learn.* San Francisco: Jossey Bass Publishers.

# NOTES

# NOTES

# NOTES

# NOTES

# NOTES

# ABOUT THE AUTHOR

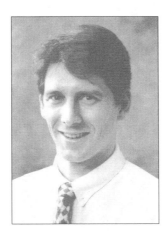

Richard J. Seibert, M.A., M.Ed., is the health promotions director at the Marine Corps Air Station Iwakuni in Japan. Seibert received his master's degree in exercise physiology from the University of Maryland, and later received a second master's degree in education from the University of Massachusetts at Boston in instructional design. He has combined these two disciplines to write study guides and articles, and create training programs for fitness professionals. Seibert has been teaching group fitness classes since 1987 and is an ACE-certified Group Fitness Instructor and Personal Trainer. As special projects manager for ACE, he designed and delivered portions of ACE's Group Exercise Practical Training Program. Seibert has presented at fitness conventions around the world and is featured in four exercise videos.

**AMERICAN COUNCIL ON EXERCISE**

*www.acefitness.org*

YES, I would like to receive information on the following ACE certifications:

❑ Lifestyle & Weight Management Consultant     ❑ Personal Trainer
❑ Group Fitness Instructor     ❑ Clinical Exercise Specialist

Name _____

Address_____

City_____ State_____ ZIP_____

Home Phone (_____)_____

Work Phone (_____)_____

E-mail _____

---

**Ace**

**AMERICAN COUNCIL ON EXERCISE**

*www.acefitness.org*

YES, I would like to receive information on the following ACE certifications:

❑ Lifestyle & Weight Management Consultant     ❑ Personal Trainer
❑ Group Fitness Instructor     ❑ Clinical Exercise Specialist

Name _____

Address_____

City_____ State_____ ZIP_____

Home Phone (_____)_____

Work Phone (_____)_____

E-mail _____

# BUSINESS REPLY MAIL
**FIRST-CLASS MAIL PERMIT NO. 22113 SAN DIEGO, CA**

POSTAGE WILL BE PAID BY ADDRESSEE

**AMERICAN COUNCIL ON EXERCISE**
**PO BOX 910449**
**SAN DIEGO CA  92191-9961**

---

# BUSINESS REPLY MAIL
**FIRST-CLASS MAIL PERMIT NO. 22113 SAN DIEGO, CA**

POSTAGE WILL BE PAID BY ADDRESSEE

**AMERICAN COUNCIL ON EXERCISE**
**PO BOX 910449**
**SAN DIEGO CA  92191-9961**